UNHERALDED STARS

WORLD TEACHERS' DAY TRIBUTE

Angel Bryan Z. Ocampo

Dedication

Dedicated

To all

TEACHERS

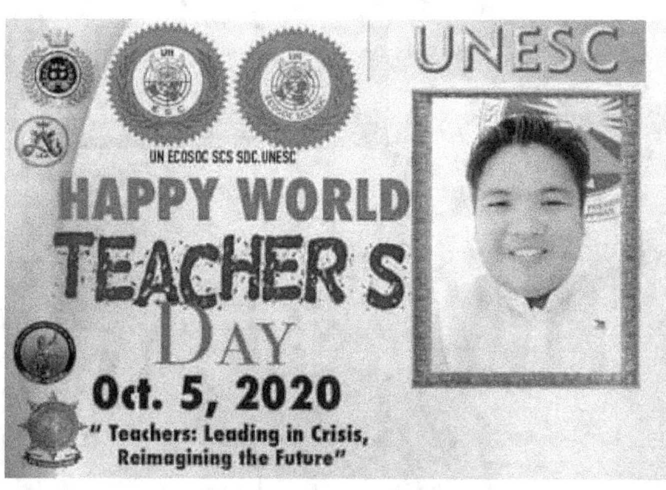

Acknowledgement

Forever Grateful

to

God,

my

shining example

and

guiding light.

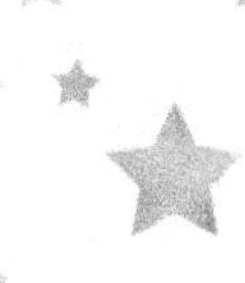

PREFACE

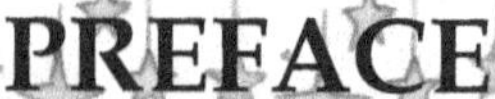

Heroes are like shining stars, their act of heroism glitters and they own the spotlight while they stand in high pedestals. But there are many heroes unrecognized by many. Among them are our dear Teachers.

Dedicated as always, their sacrifices and heroism do not just happen once for all time but for as long as they live. Others clearly recognize these but people in general often take them for granted ignoring the fact that they played a huge part in the lives of each individual, honing unnumbered ones to success. Angel Bryan's book has been prepared unselfishly to spread, highlight and remind us, that we have been surrounded by these wonderful heroes…

Angel Bryan Ocampo's book will give us a glimpse of himself, not only as a teacher, who is highly respected and beloved, but also as someone reflecting many facets of beautiful rays from within. His book will inspire us as we discover his many awesome qualities. Kindness, despite its rarity in today's world, it does blossom from him elating our hearts to love this hero. Modesty, while it is man's instinct to brag about his achievements and

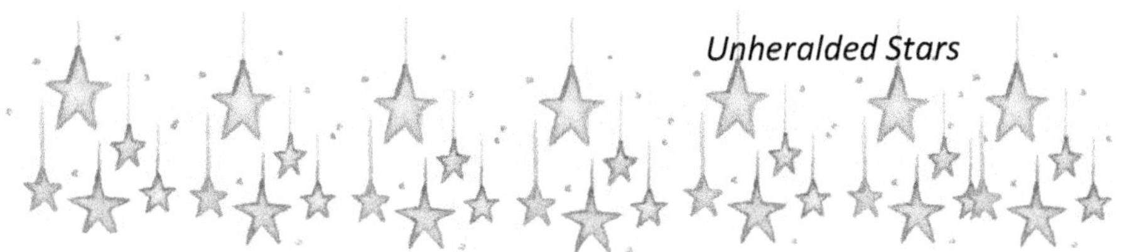

talents, Angel has been endowed with humility viewing others higher than him addressing them "Ma'am and Sir", regardless of their position in society. Generosity, proving true the words "there indeed is greater happiness in giving". He gives wholeheartedly expecting nothing in return.

Teacher Angel Bryan Z. Ocampo indeed deserves our salute as He shines brightly unceasingly into the lives of many.. You, too will be refreshed by his awesomeness... Read his book and you will find out yourself.

The Publisher

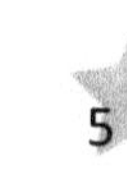

CONTENTS

World Teachers' Day

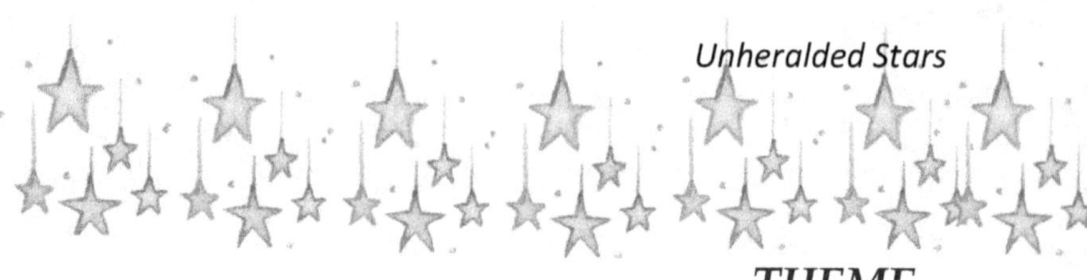

THEME...

TEACHERS: LEADING IN CRISIS, REIMAGINING THE FUTURE
2020

Teachers lead the way as the frontliners of education. Amidst pandemic, education must not stop. Learning must continue. Teachers make way for their learners to learn.

The future lies in their hands. The future becomes clearer for their students.

TEACHER...

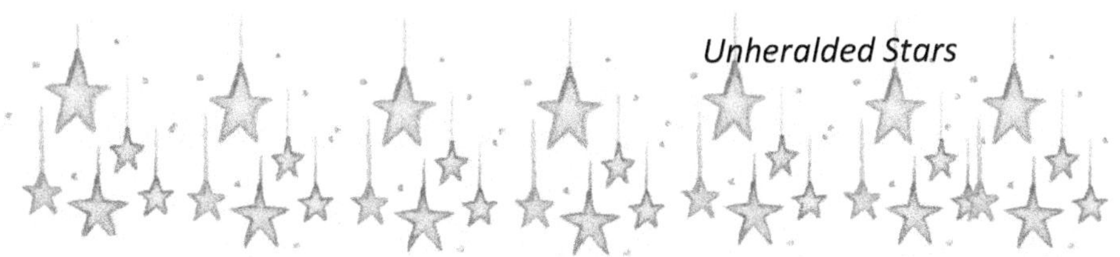

THEME...

YOUNG TEACHERS: THE FUTURE OF THE PROFESSION
2019

Young once will soon leave the profession. Young ones are expected to take the lead as the new breed of teachers. With the drive to create a change, young teachers, indeed, are the future of the profession.

In this digital era, these young teachers have all the resources to redeem the profession.

TEACHER...

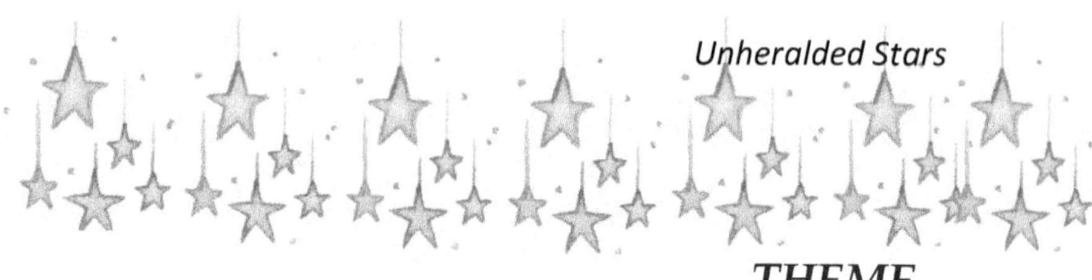

THE RIGHT TO EDUCATION MEANS THE RIGHT TO A QUALIFIED TEACHER
2018

Quality education depends on the quality of teachers produced and hired. Teachers must be qualified for what s/he knows not only whom s/he knows.

The right to education will only be given justice if the teacher is qualified to teach.

TEACHER...

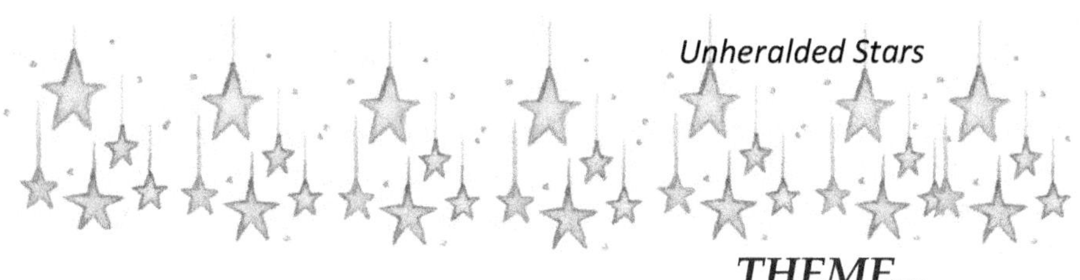

THEME...

TEACHING IN FREEDOM, EMPOWERING TEACHERS
2017

Our mission is to break the chain of ignorance among our learners. We must provide them quality and liberating education.

We can never give our students the education they deserve if our teachers are not empowered to use his/her God-given skills.

TEACHER...

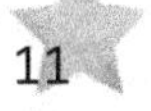

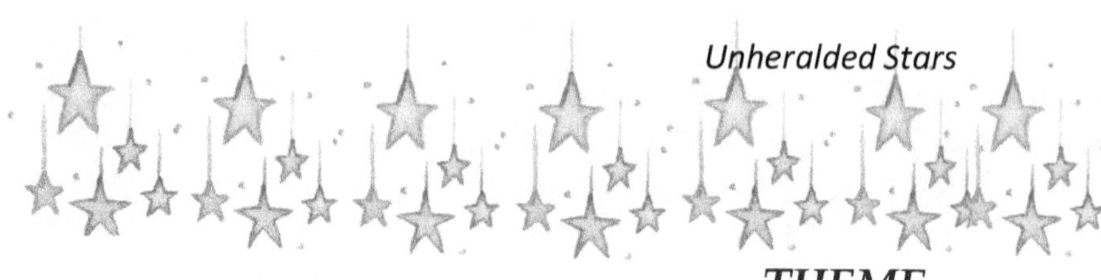

THEME...

VALUING TEACHERS, IMPROVING THEIR STATUS
2016

An authority said, "We can never put our students first if we put our teachers last."

Teachers' status in the society should be given importance. They deserve to be appreciated and recognized.

To boost their morale means to care for students.

TEACHER...

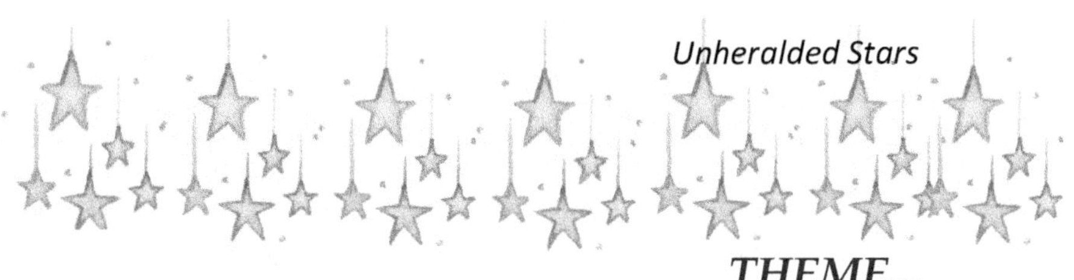

THEME...

EMPOWERING TEACHERS, BUILDING SUSTAINABLE SOCIETIES
2015

To empower is to build. To demoralize is to destroy.

Stop Bullying, Stop Blaming Teachers is one key factor to build a strong harmonious community.

Teachers play a vital role in the formation of sustainable society. They mold the future of the nation.

TEACHER...

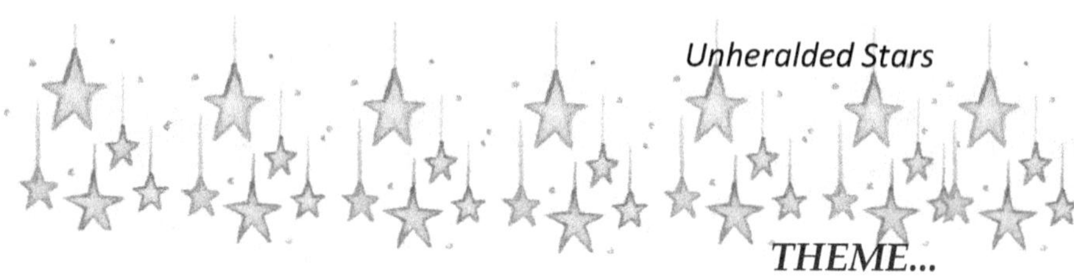

INVEST IN THE FUTURE, INVEST IN TEACHERS
2014

Investment in education is the most productive thing to do. Thus, investing in teachers is also investing in the future.

Teachers should be given equal opportunities to grow and live a comfortable life. If teachers don't receive a decent life, the performance is affected.

TEACHER...

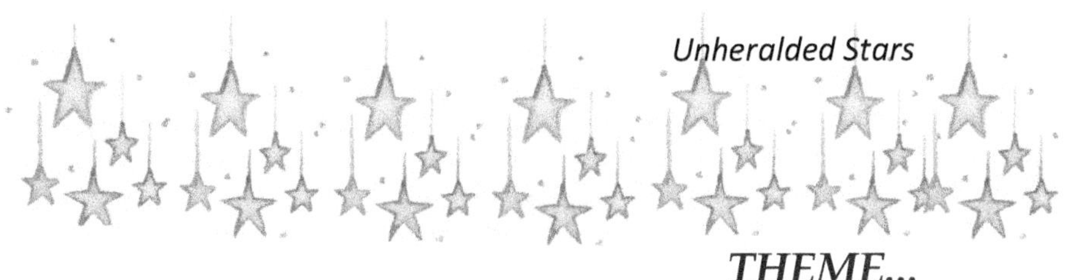

THEME...

A CALL FOR TEACHERS
2013

Many are called but few are chosen.

Teaching is the greatest calling. This is a calling where a person gives his everything – his time, resources, skills, talents and even himself.

It's a call for teachers to redeem the profession.

To regain its throne as the noblest profession.

TEACHER...

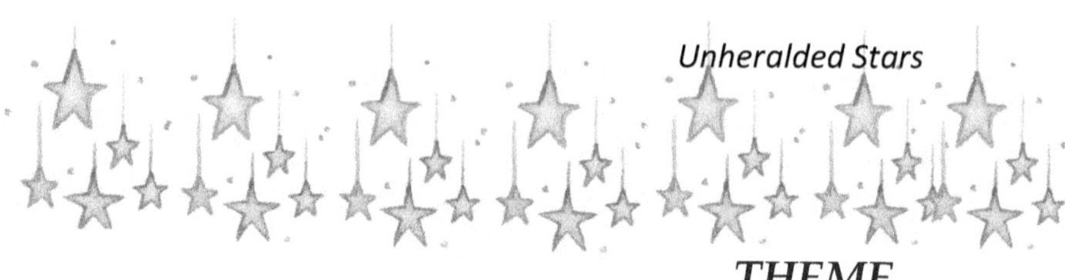

THEME...

TAKE A STAND FOR TEACHERS
2012

Who will be the voice of teachers when they become voiceless?

Who will be their ears when no one listens?

Who will be their hands when they need help?

Who will be their feet if they can't stand anymore?

Fight for teachers! Stand Up for them!

TEACHER...

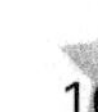

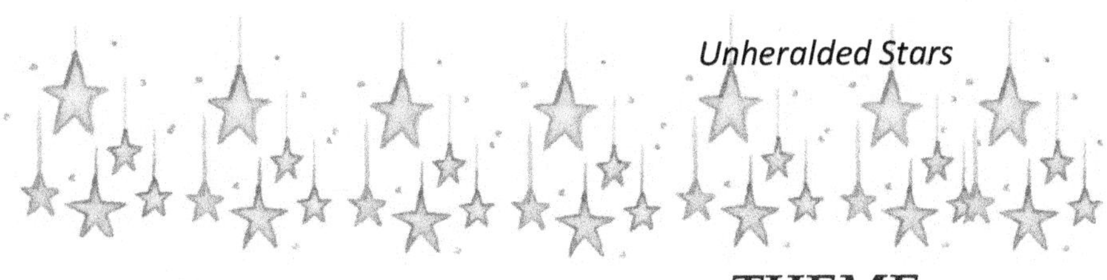

THEME...

TEACHERS FOR GENDER EQUALITY
2011

R	–	E	–	S	–	P
–	E	–	C	–	T	

Teachers respect gender equality. Each is unique. Each has his/her own individuality. Each is special.

Gender should not solely be the basis of a person's worth.

As the line of the song goes, every color, every hue is represented by me and you.

TEACHER...

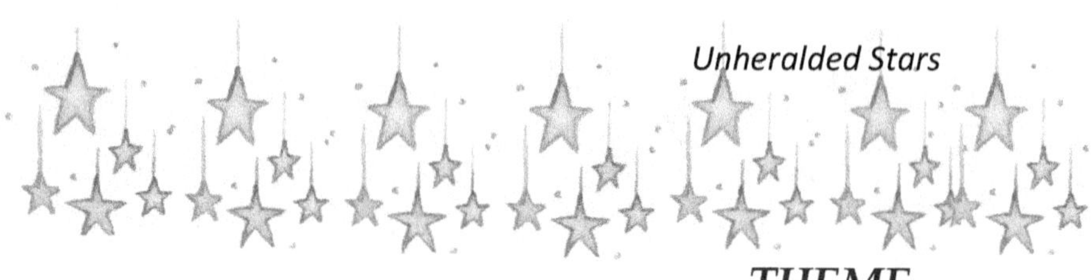

THEME...

MY TEACHER, MY HERO
2010

Teachers are unsung heroes. They play different roles in the lives of their students.

As the saying goes, for others you may just be a teacher, but for your students you are their heroes.

Don't stop doing good for your students because we have no idea how much you have touched their lives.

TEACHER...

BITUING WALANG NINGNING

BITUIN...

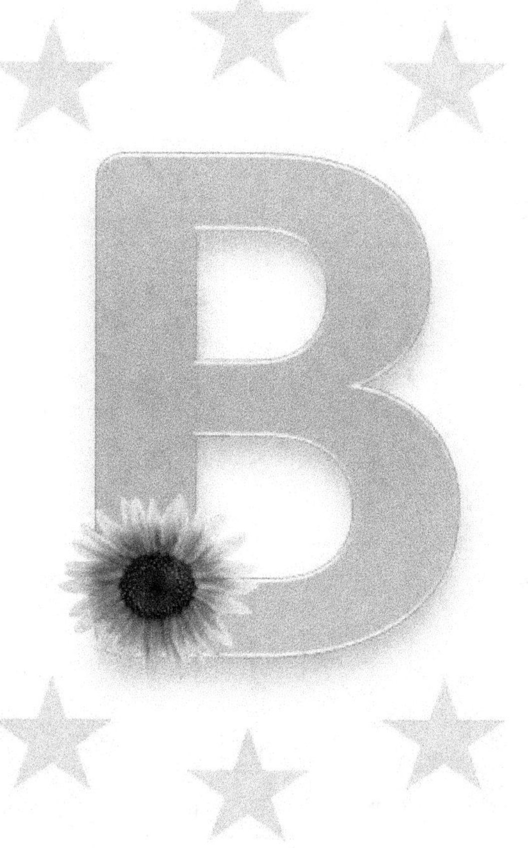

TEACHER...

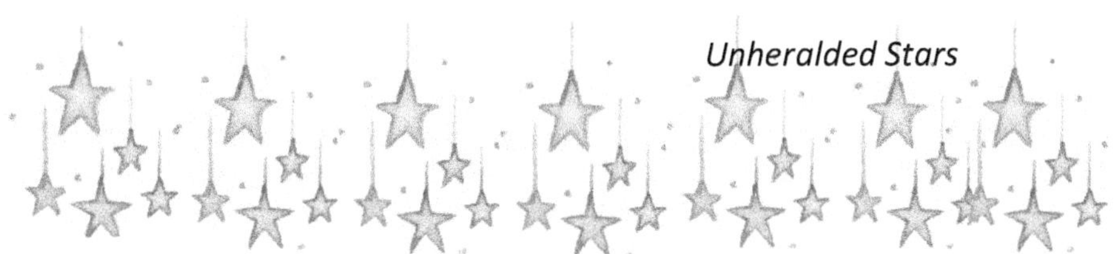

Backpack

Like a bag full of things.

Teachers have full of responsibilities but they carry them well.

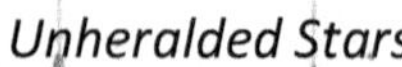

Bituin...

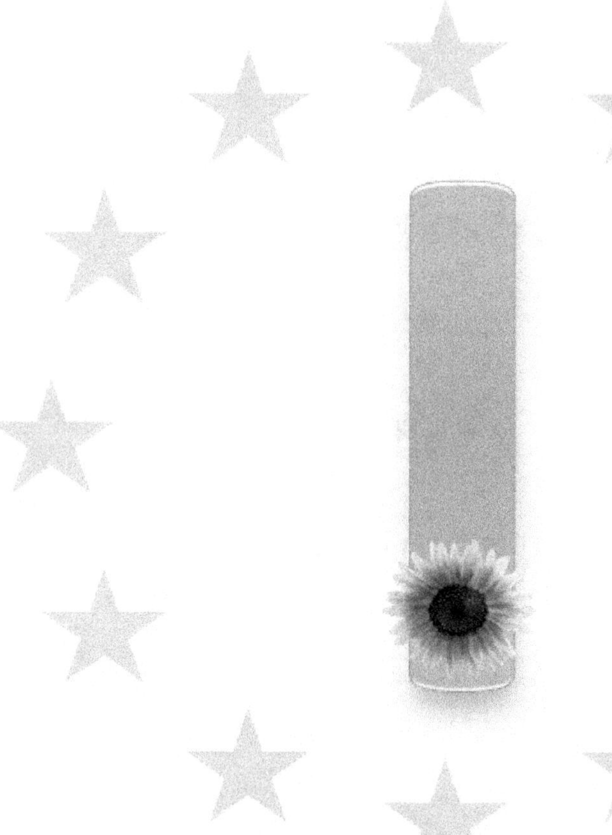

TEACHER...

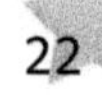

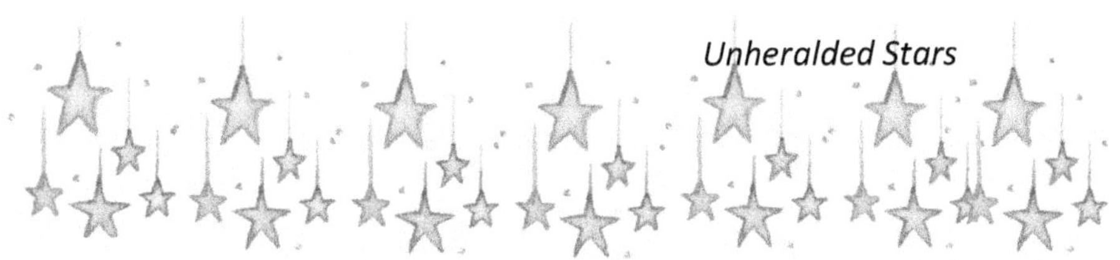

Ink

Like an ink that can be
consumed.

Teachers, too, get
exhausted but they leave
an indelible mark.

B ITUIN...

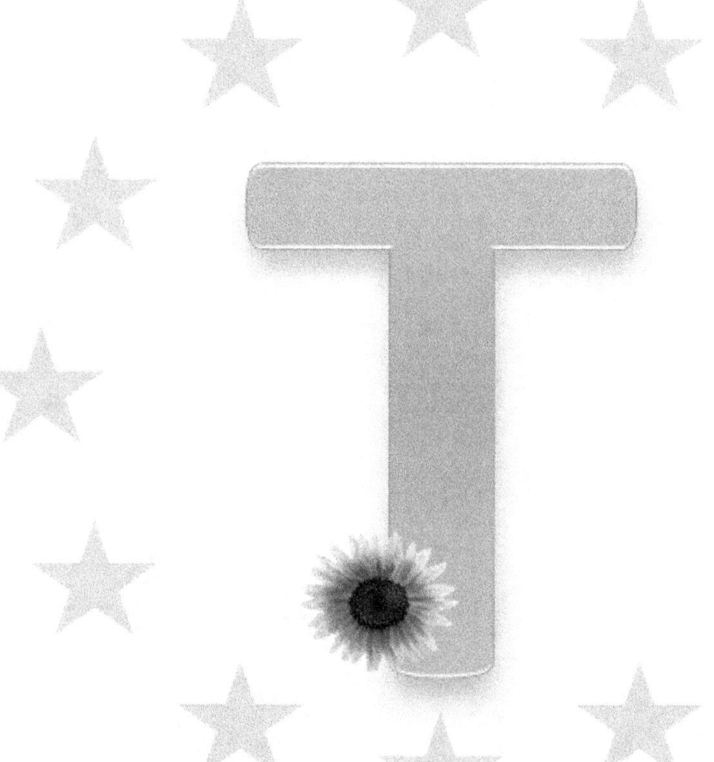

TEACHER...

TEST PAPER

Like a test paper that can be easy or hard.

Teachers are sometimes tender or tough but they teach lesson from the heart.

BITUIN...

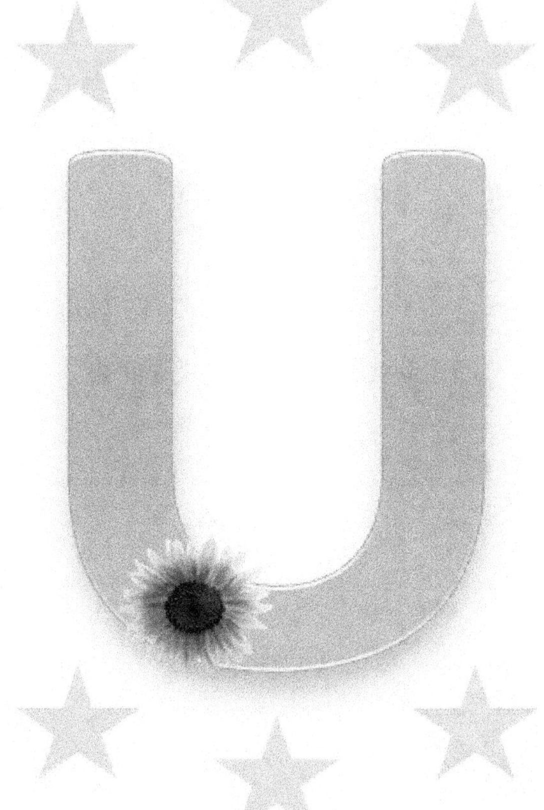

TEACHER...

UMBRELLA

Like an umbrella, rain or
shine, is useful.

Teachers have their own
problems but they
remain supportive in
good times or hard times.

B ITUIN...

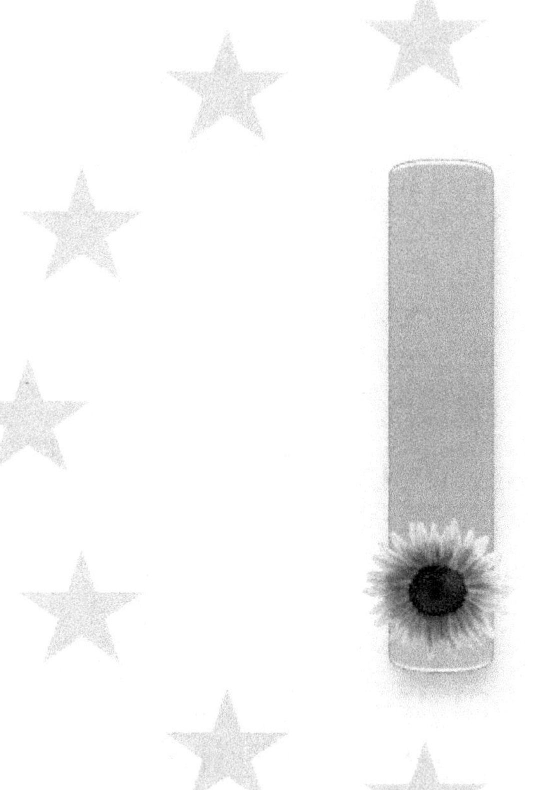

TEACHER...

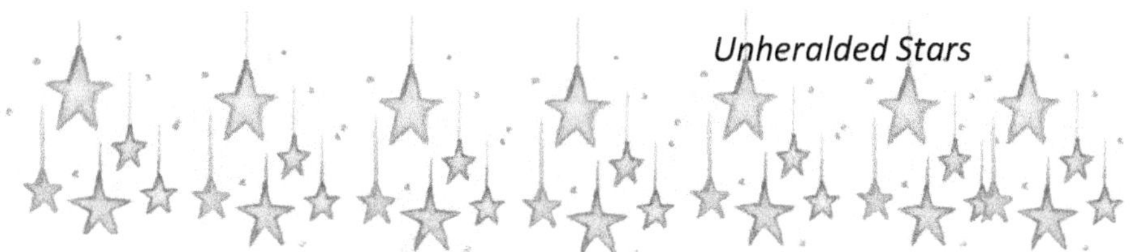

ICE CREAM

Like an ice cream cold
and delicious.

Teachers, too, get mad
but they remain sweet
and never give cold
shoulders.

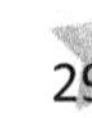

BITUIN...

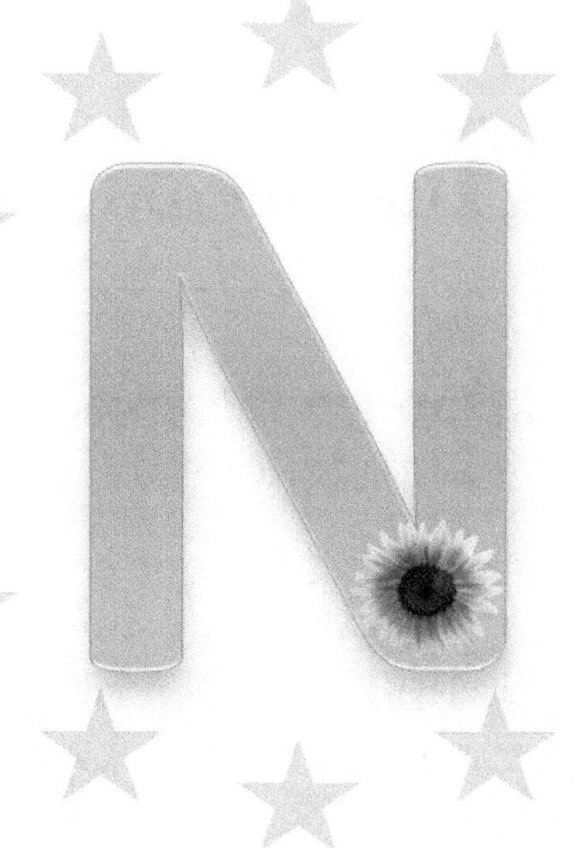

TEACHER...

NOTEBOOK

Like a notebook space for
notes.

Teachers' advice
sometimes taken for
granted but they send
messages from the heart
and notes to life.

BITUIN...

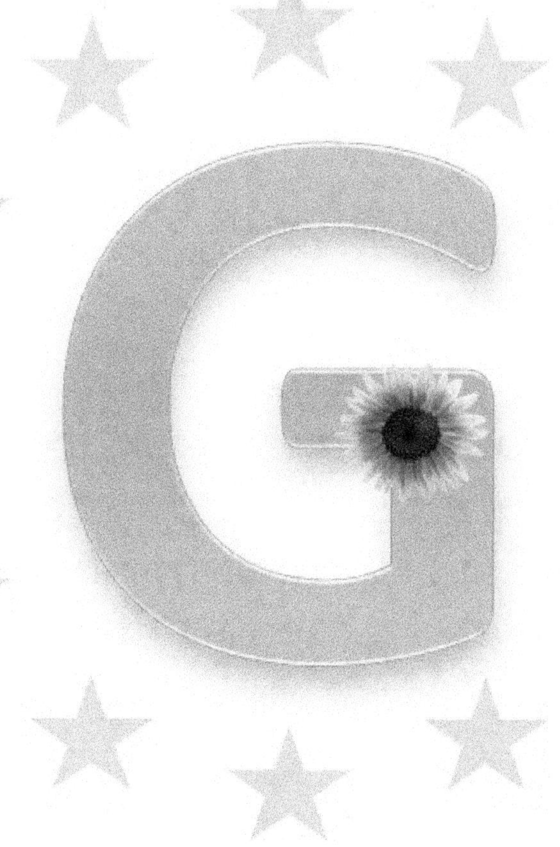

TEACHER...

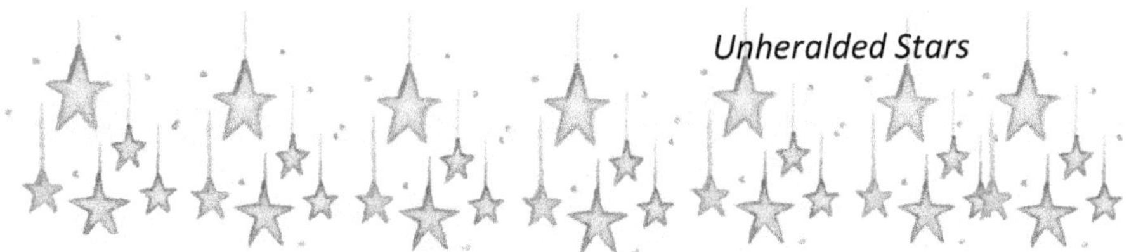

GOOGLE

Like a google source of information.

Teachers are not only provider of information but also the molder of characters.

BITUIN...

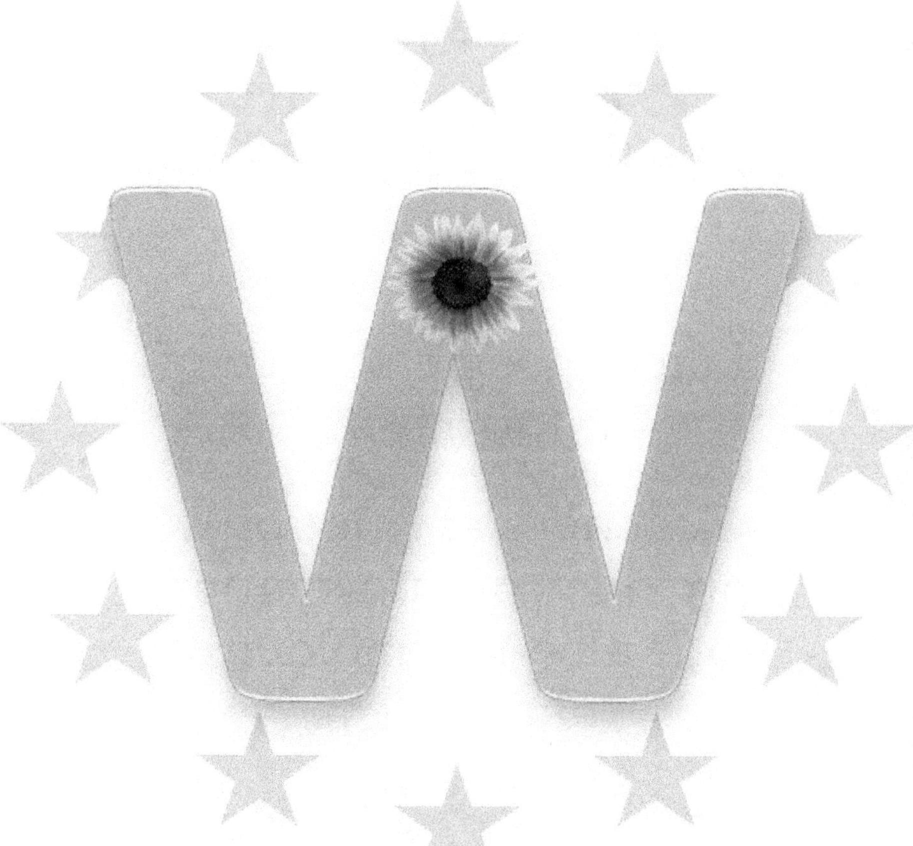

W

TEACHER...

WRISTWATCH

Like a wristwatch that
works 24/7.

Teachers work overtime
but they do it quietly.

BITUIN...

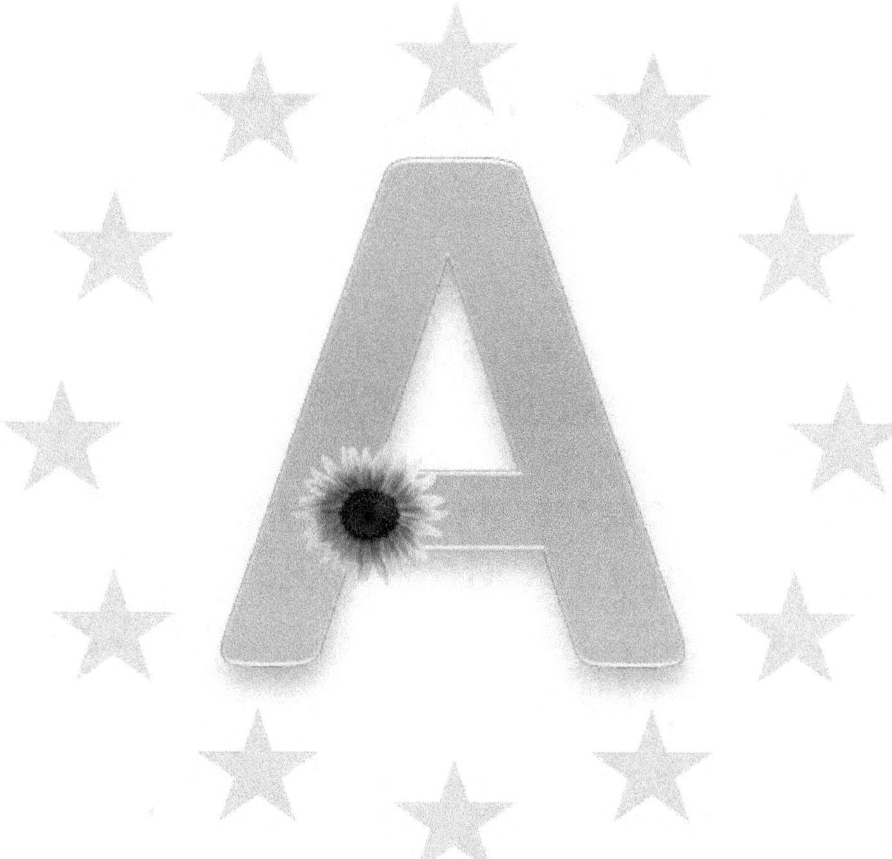

A

TEACHER...

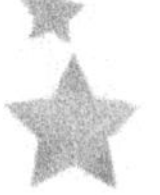

APPLE

Like an apple that keeps
the doctor away.

Teachers do get sick but
they still teach to cure
the ignorance.

BITUIN...

TEACHER...

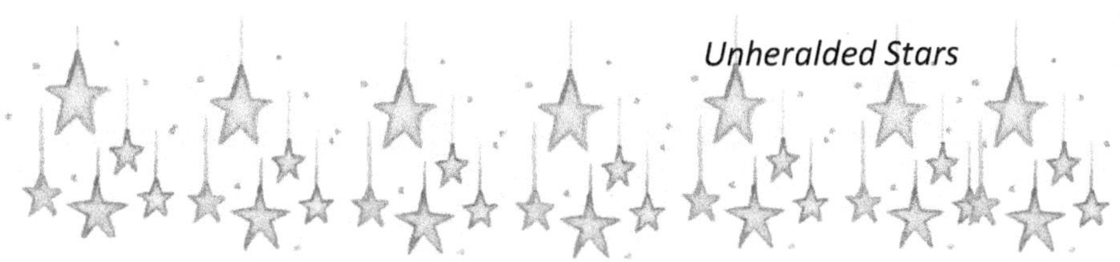

LAPTOP

Like a laptop that
multitasks.

Teachers juggle different
things but they can still
multitask with
excellence.

BITUIN...

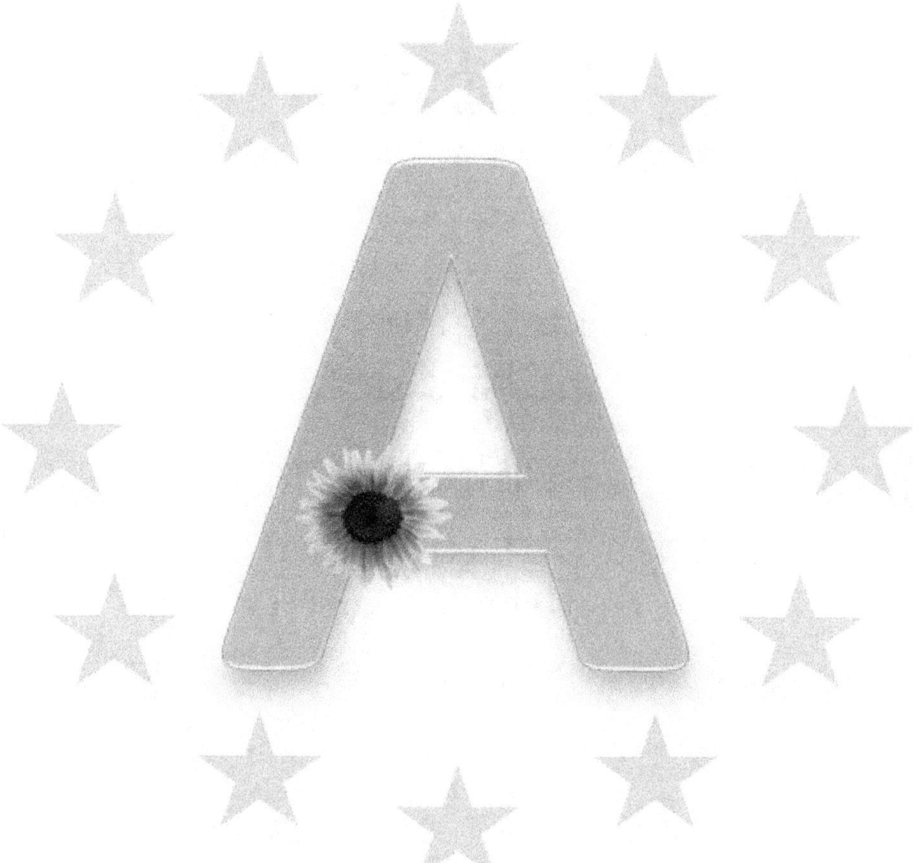

A

TEACHER...

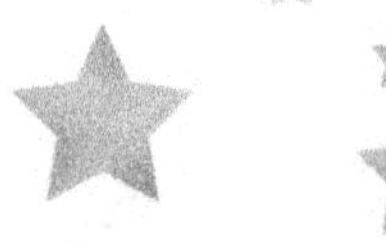

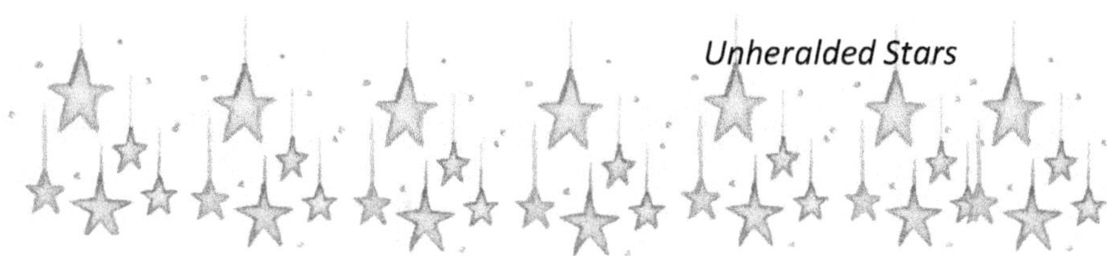

ANGELS

Like guardian angels we
don't see.

Teachers still receive
disrespectful remarks
but they remain
students' silent angels.

Bituin...

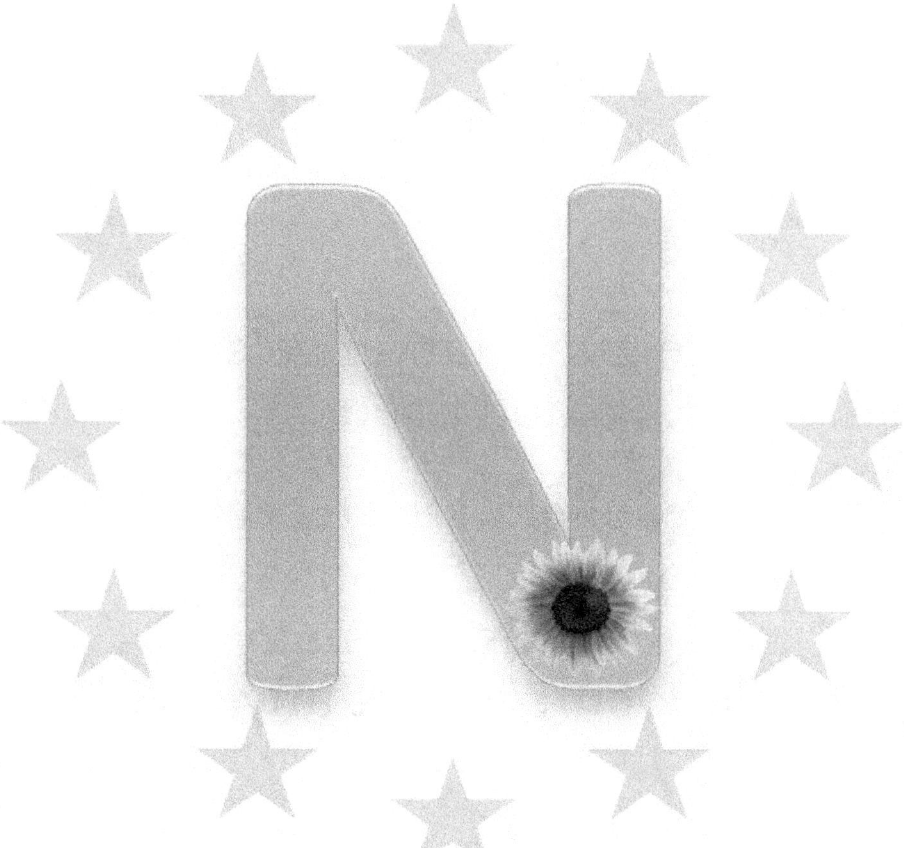

N

TEACHER...

NUMBERS

Like numbers we learn to
count.

Teachers face also
challenges in life but we
can still count on them.

Bituin...

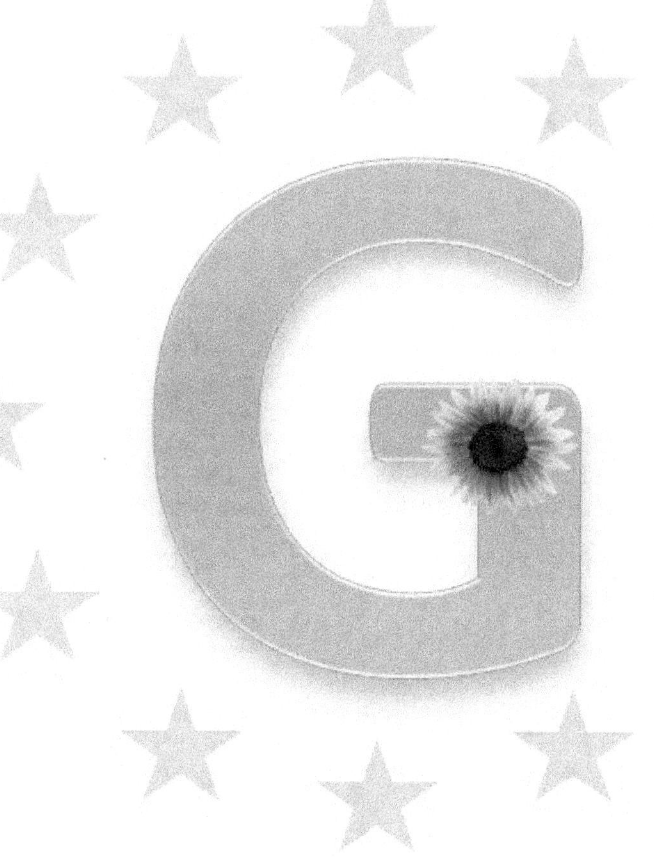

TEACHER...

GLUE

Like a glue that sticks.

Teachers are busy people
but they stick together
through thick and thin.

BITUIN...

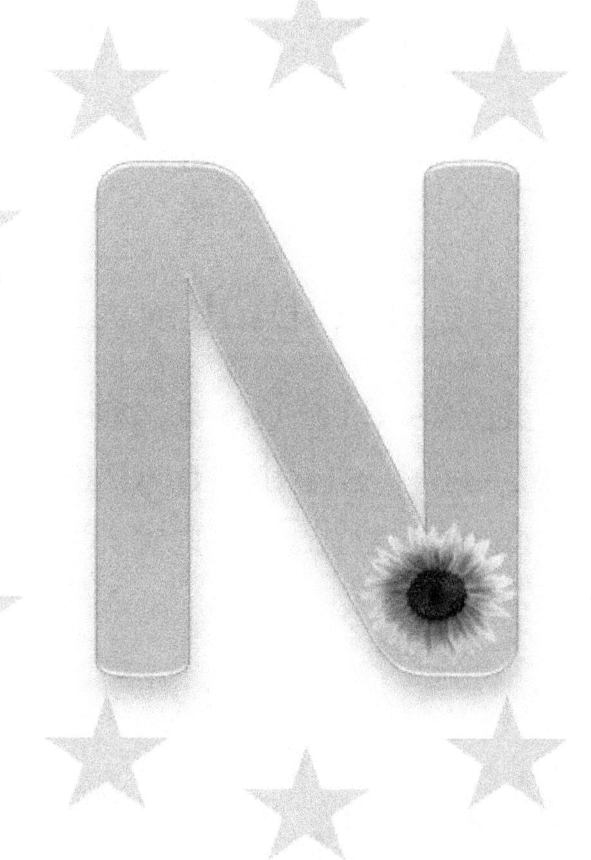

TEACHER...

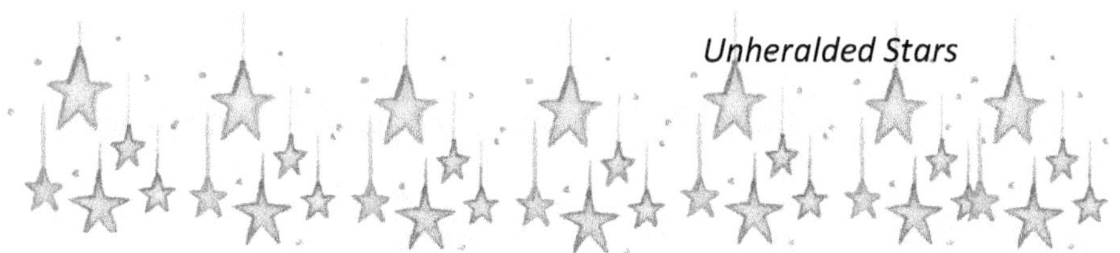

NINE

Like a nine in a cloud so lucky.

Teachers are not only lucky but also blessed despite being underpaid.

BITUIN...

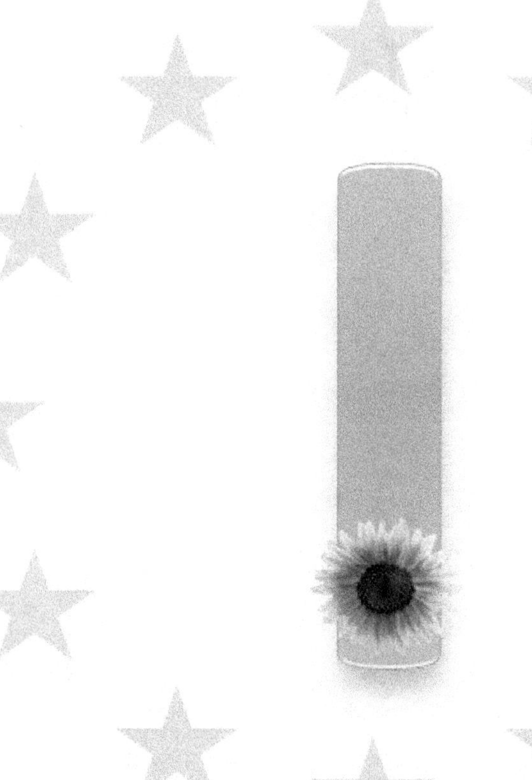

TEACHER...

INSTAGRAM

Like an instagram
capturing photos.

Teachers are
unrecognized and
unsung but they have
beautiful photos of
moments with their
students to treasure.

BITUIN...

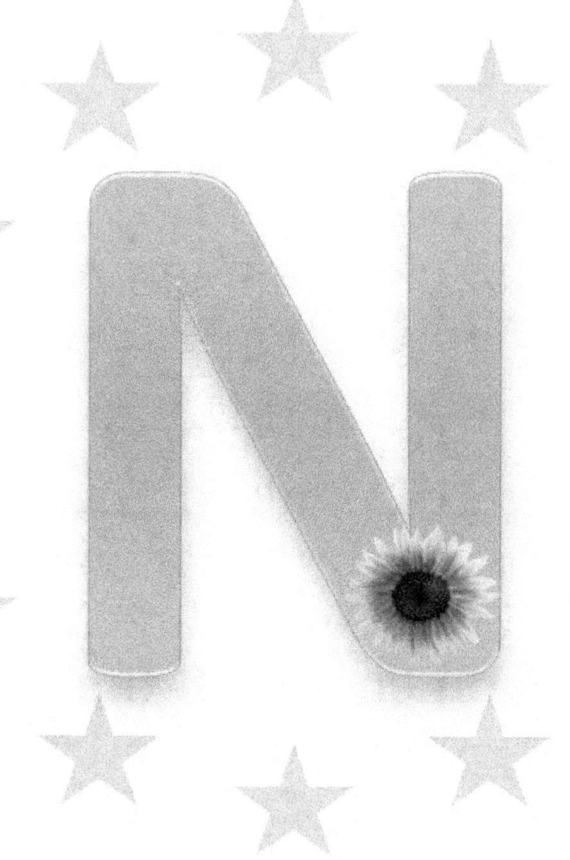

TEACHER...

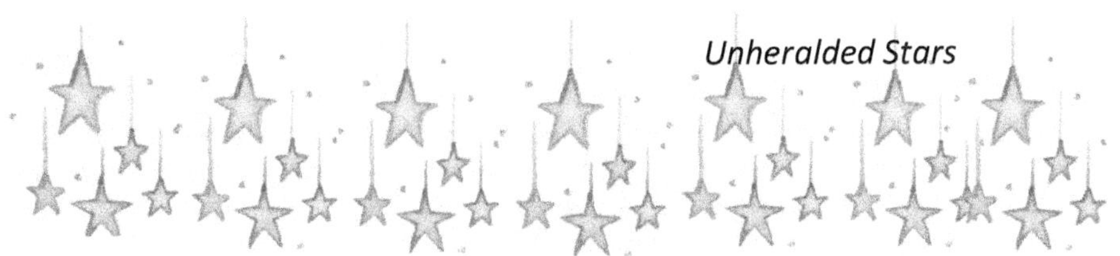

Names

Like names remembered
and forgotten.

Teachers are nameless in
the limelight but they
still work for others to
shine.

BITUIN...

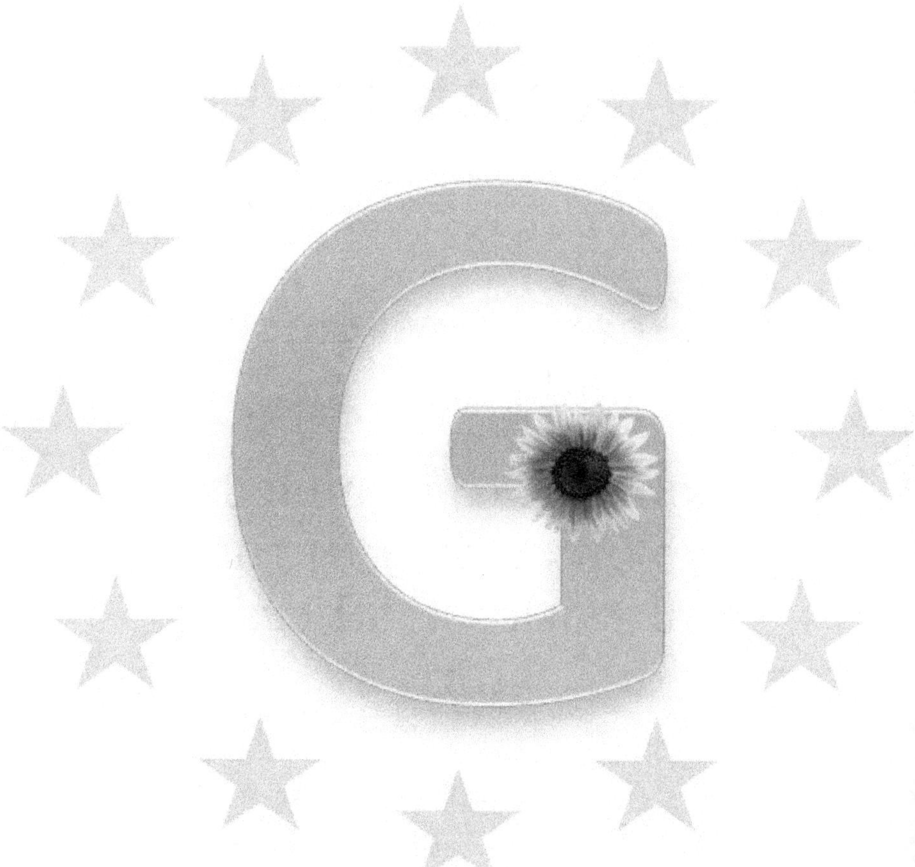

G

TEACHER...

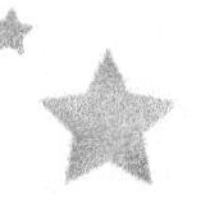

GIFTS

Like a gift unwrapped.

Teachers are
unappreciated
individuals but they
remain beautiful gifts
that bring happiness to
the world.

BITUIN..

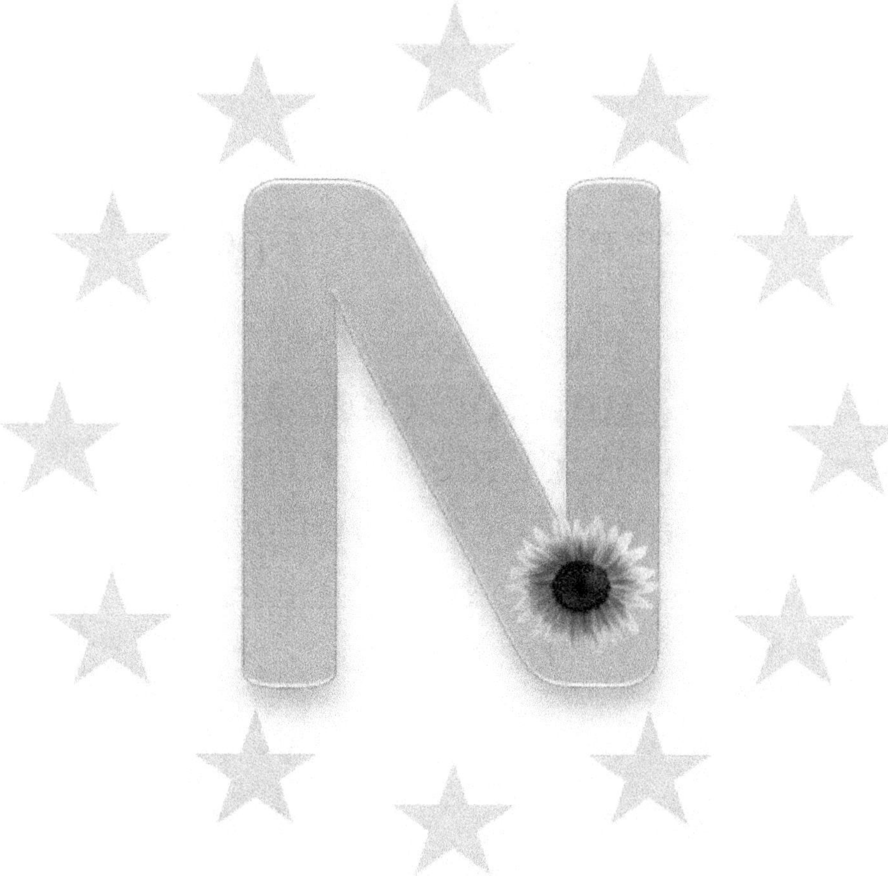

N

TEACHER...

NIGHT

Like a night to unveil.

Teachers experience
cloudy situation
especially this pandemic
but they still manage to
give light and show the
beauty of life hidden in
darkness.

BITUIN...

TEACHER...

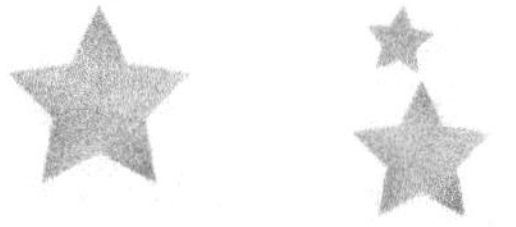

INVITE CARD

Like an invitation card
unanswered.

Teachers experience
rejection from others but
they still keep on helping
and reaching out.

Bituin...

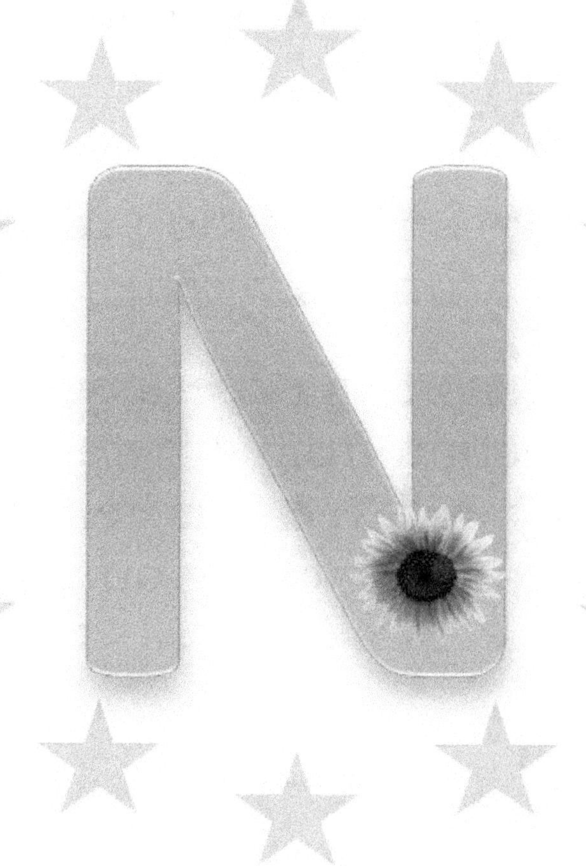

TEACHER...

Nest

Like a nest a nursing
haven for eggs.

Teachers are overworked
but they still
wholeheartedly care for
and nurture children.

B ITUIN...

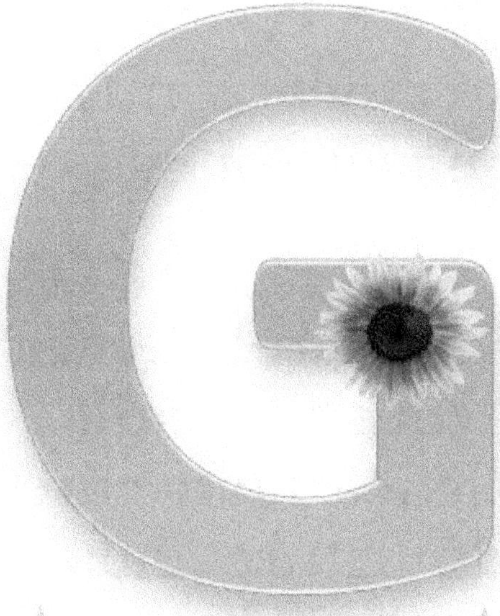

G

TEACHER...

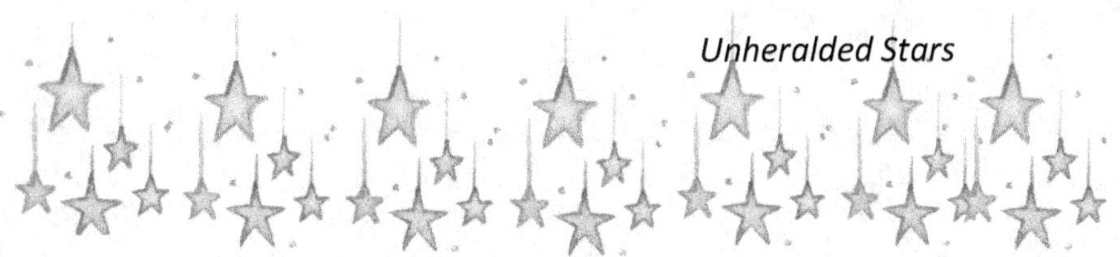

GATE

Like a gate with
entrances and exits.

Teachers' entrances and
exits remain unnoticed
but they still do their job
with passion.

UNHERALDED
STAR

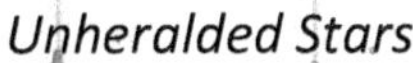

STAR...

U

TEACHER...

UBIQUITOUS

Jesus himself, the greatest teacher is ubiquitous.

This pandemic, teachers' presence is still felt everywhere via Distance Learning modality.

S TAR...

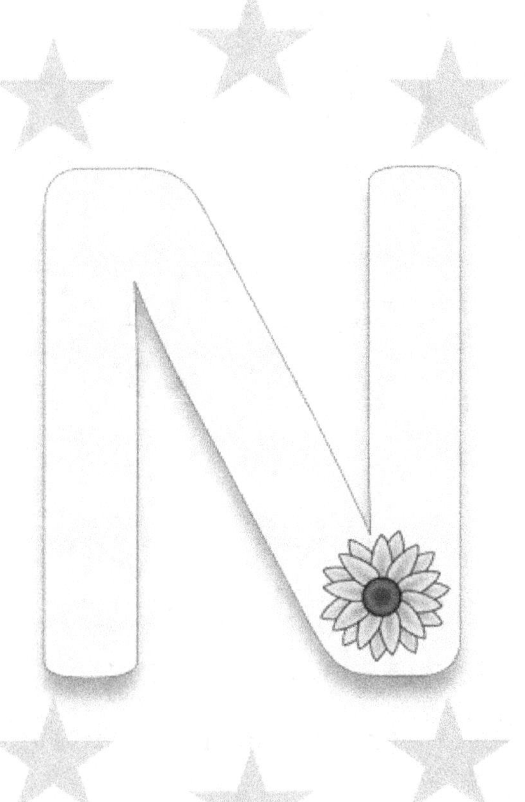

TEACHER...

NOBLEST

Teaching is the noblest profession.

This pandemic, teachers' nobility is still seen through their work at home arrangement.

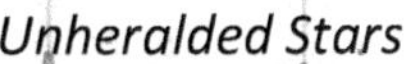

STAR...

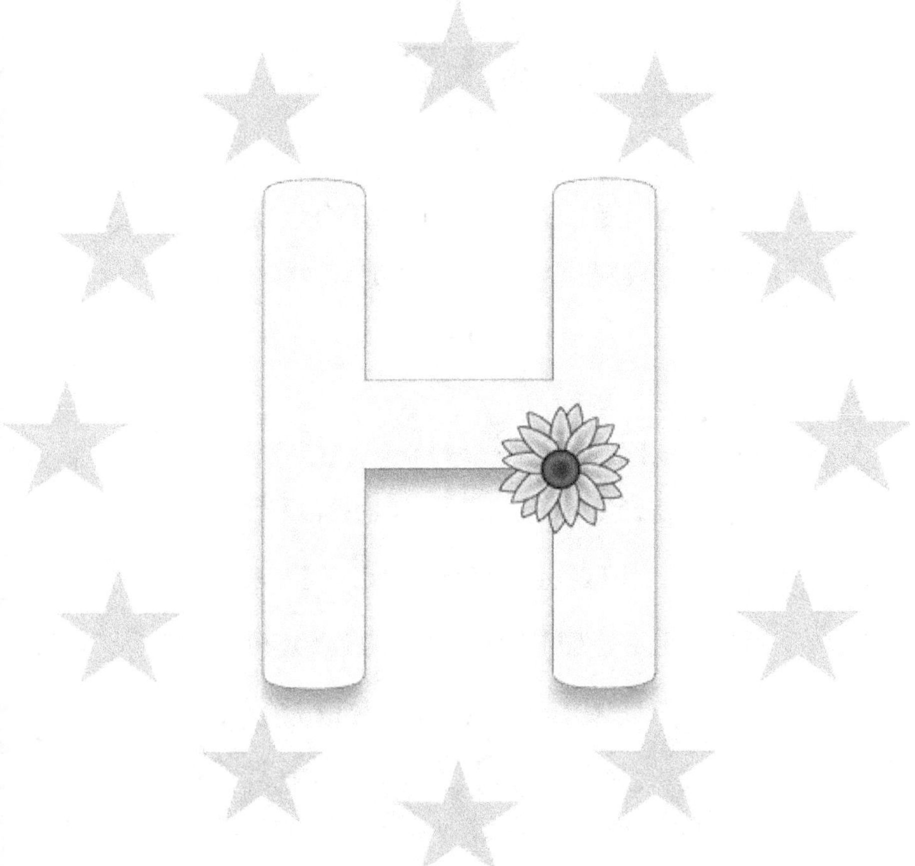

H

TEACHER...

Heroic

TeacHeroes are the proof of not all heroes wear capes.

This pandemic, teachers' heroic deeds are manifested in distributing of modules by reaching to students in a far-flung areas.

STAR...

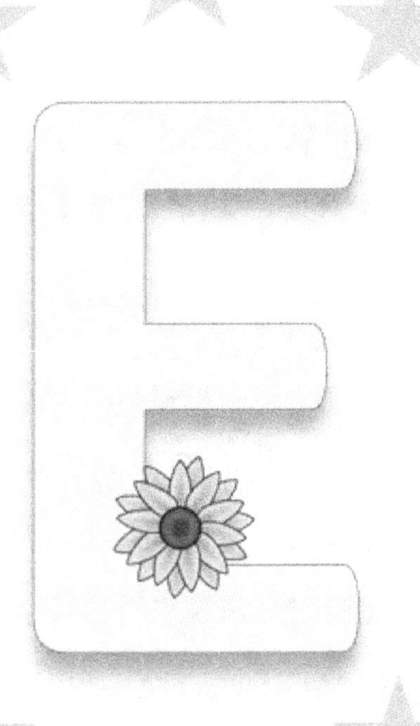

TEACHER...

Empowered

Empowered Teachers empower their students.

This pandemic, teachers' power to empower is evident through their community partnerships with stakeholders, parents and others.

STAR...

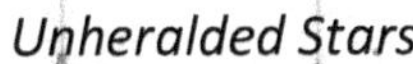

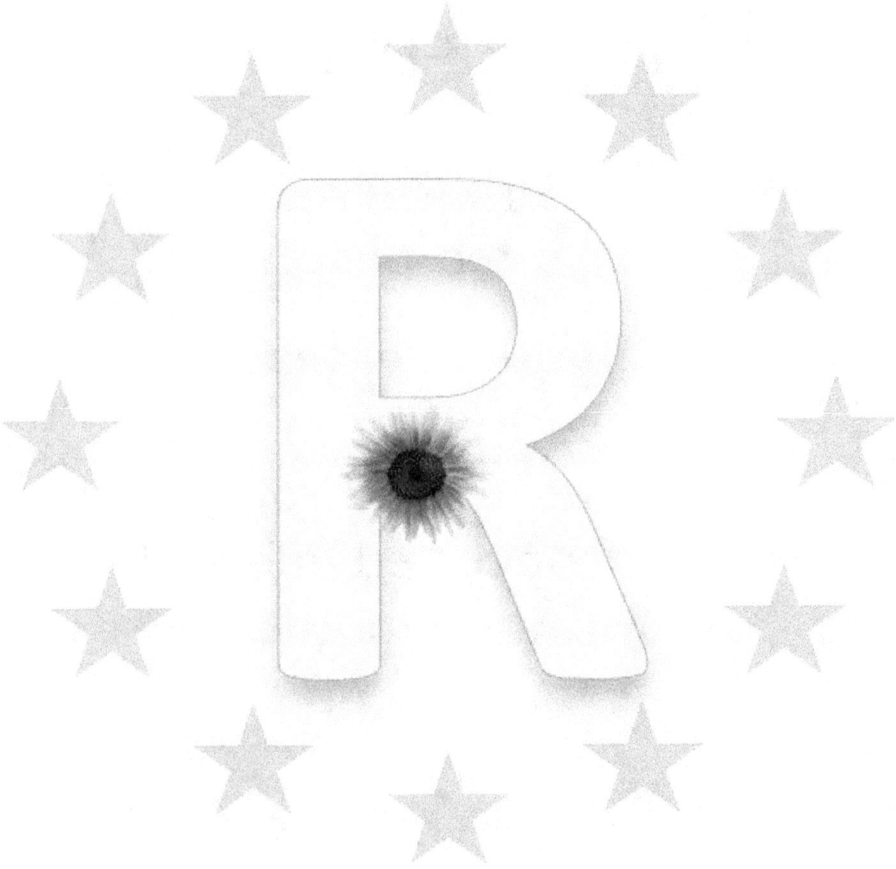

R

TEACHER...

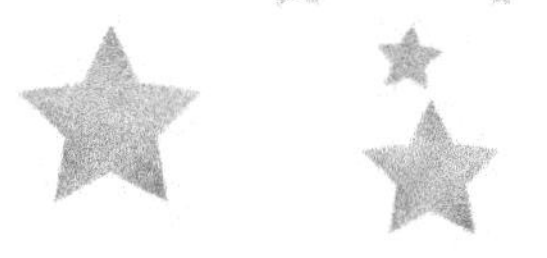

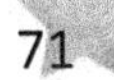

RESULT-ORIENTED

Teachers are result-oriented people.

This pandemic, teachers make education possible for students through their concerted effort of printing modules.

STAR...

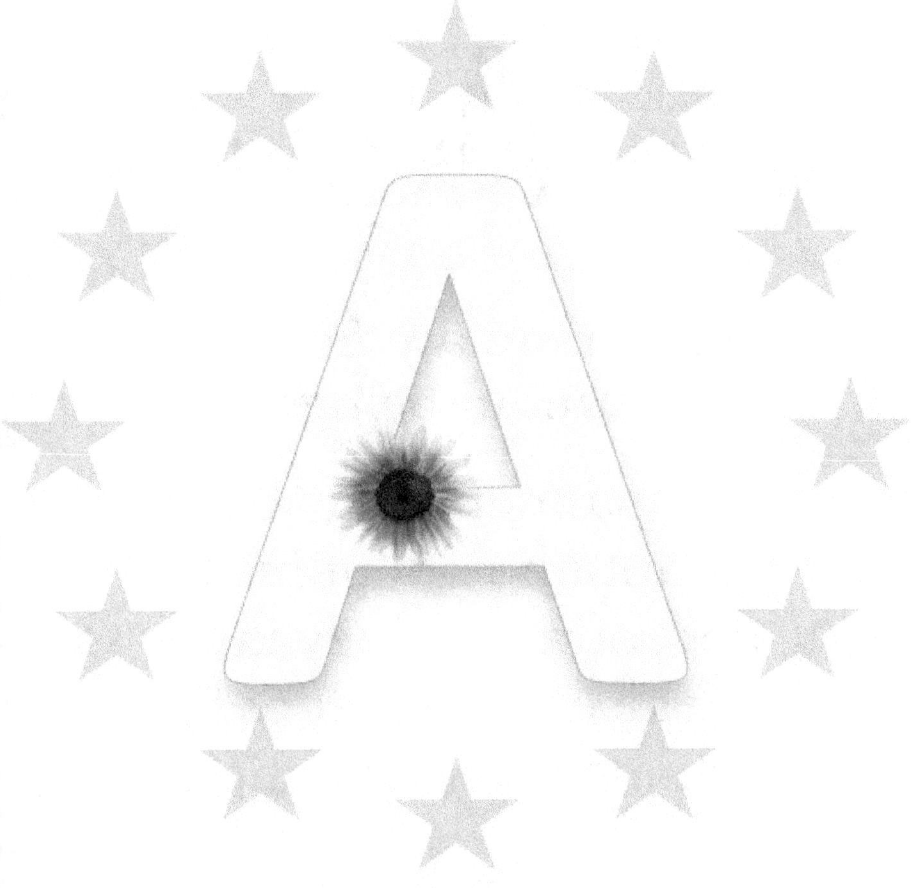

A

TEACHER...

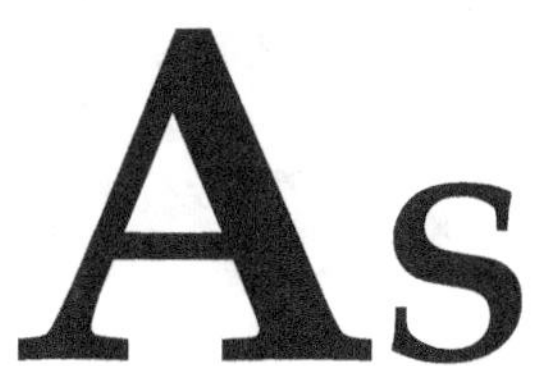

As

Teachers are flexible human beings.

This pandemic, teachers' adapt and adopt in the new normal. They make themselves adept of the changes in education.

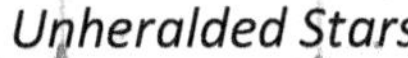

STAR...

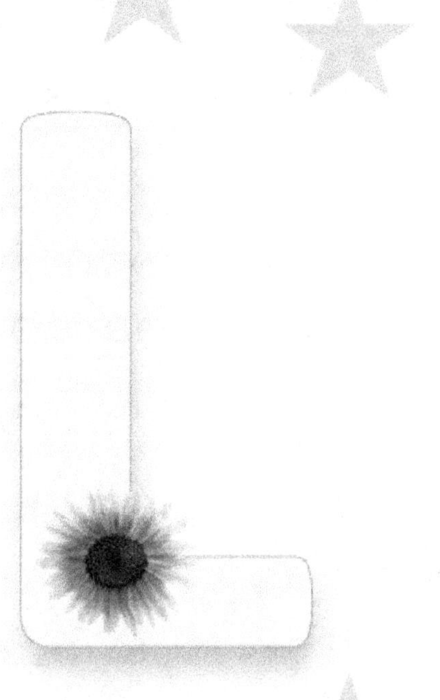

TEACHER...

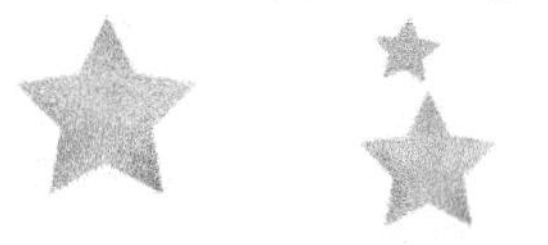

LOVING

Teachers' loving ways is incomparable.

This pandemic, teachers share a part of their salary to give relief goods to the most affected families.

Star...

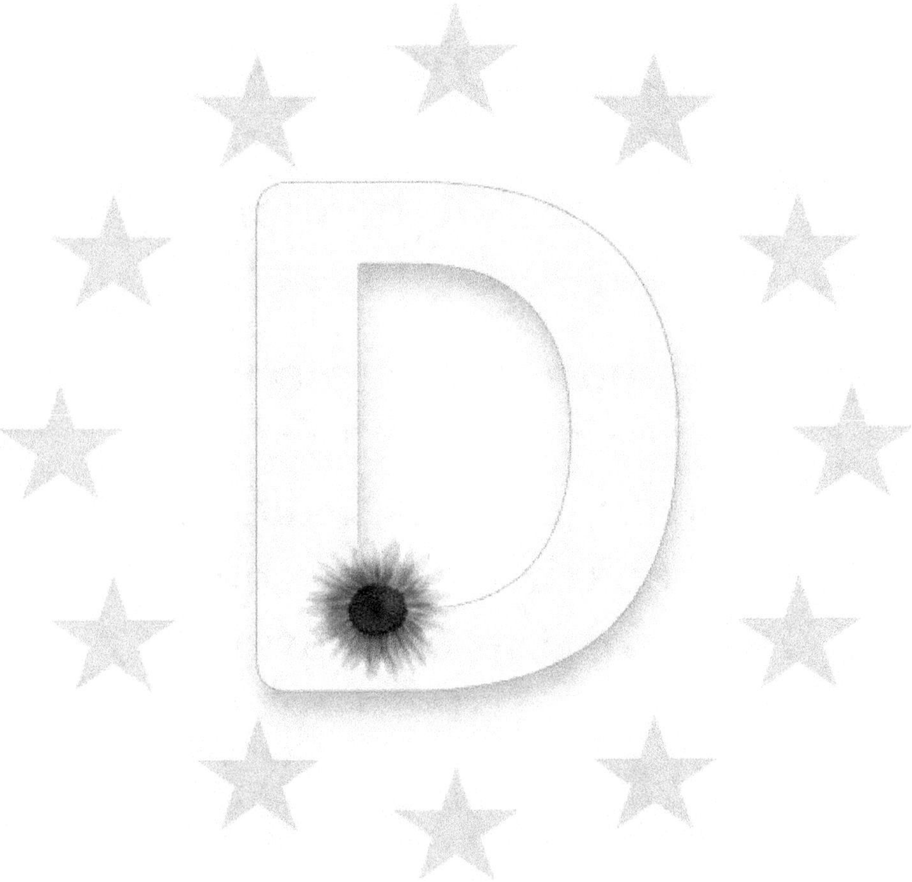

TEACHER...

DEDICATED

Teachers' dedication is beyond compare.

This pandemic, teachers devote their time, strength and skills in preparing for the new normal in education.

Star...

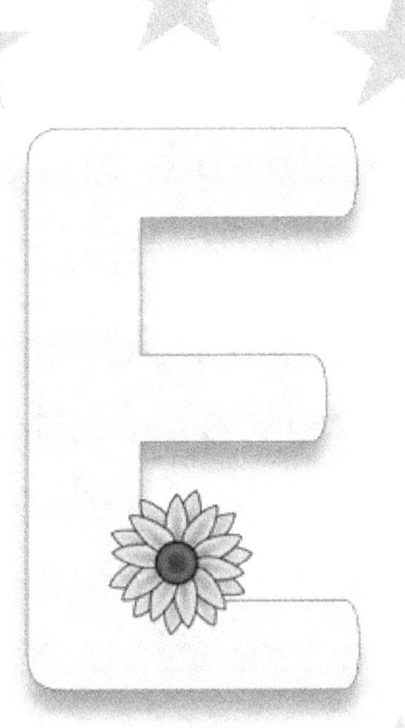

TEACHER...

EXCELLENT

Excellence equates Teachers.

This pandemic, teachers effectively and efficiently use their God-given talents to deliver quality education for

SY 2020-2021.

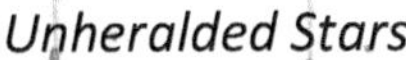

STAR...

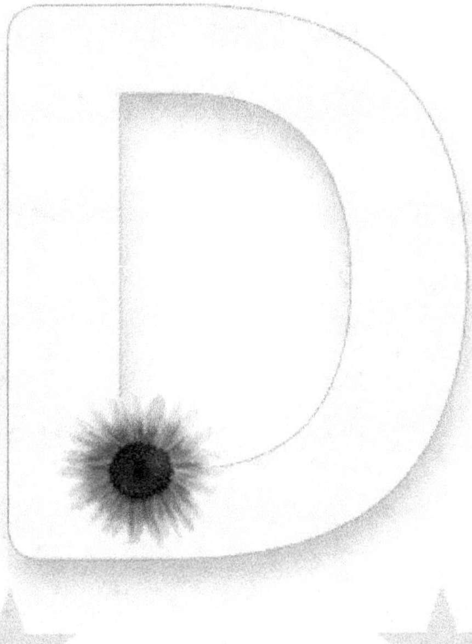

D

TEACHER...

DISCIPLINED

Teachers are disciplined professionals.

This pandemic, teachers follow the lockdown rules and obey the health and safety protocols.

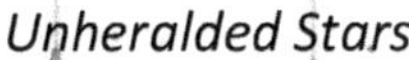

STAR...

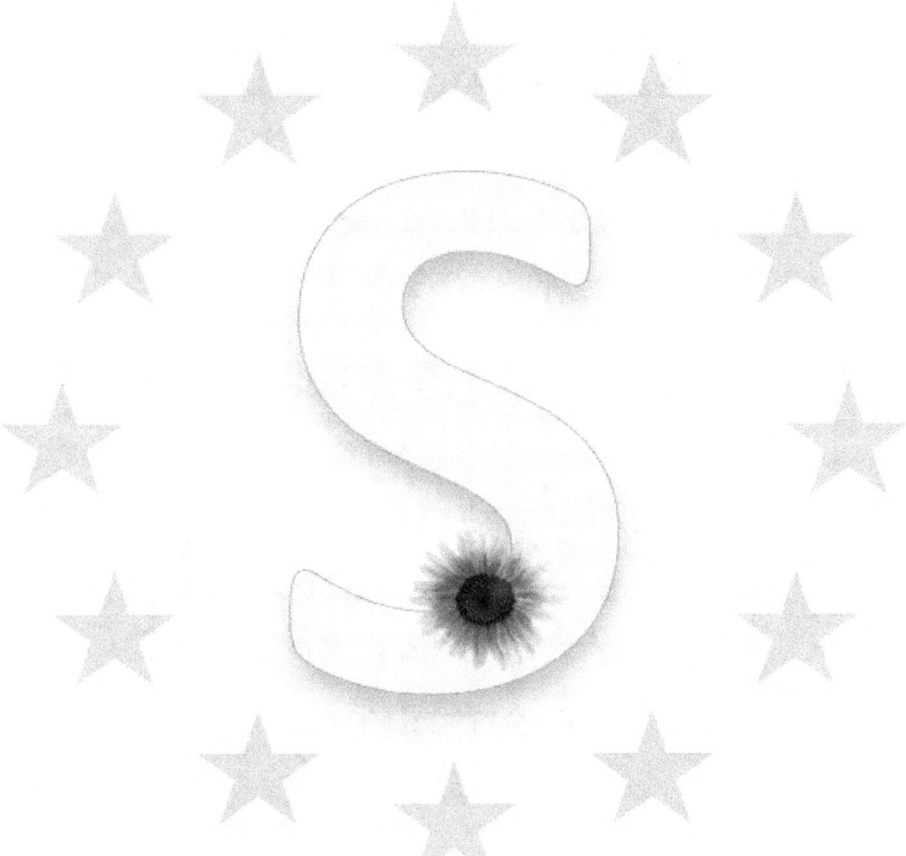

TEACHER...

Surrogate

Teachers are the second parents.

This pandemic, teachers remain surrogate parents to their learners. They keep on reminding their students to take care of themselves.

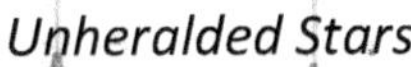

S TAR...

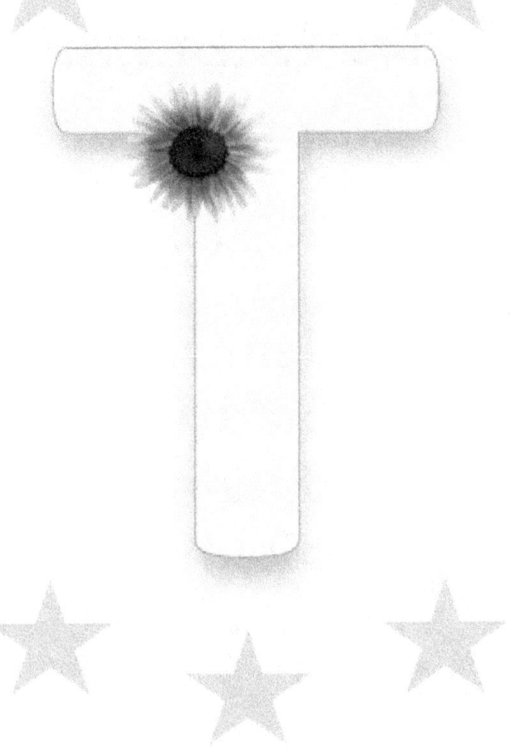

TEACHER...

TIMELESS

Teachers' influence is endless.

This pandemic, teachers remain enduring. Their contribution in the community has never stopped.

STAR...

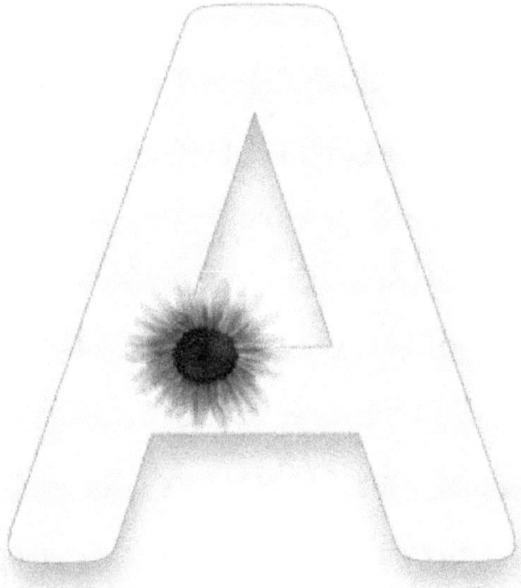

A

TEACHER...

ADJECTIVES

Teachers are like adjectives.

This pandemic, teachers' role remain superlative. There are many descriptive words to describe their work.

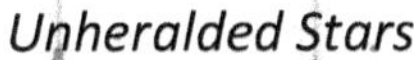

S TAR...

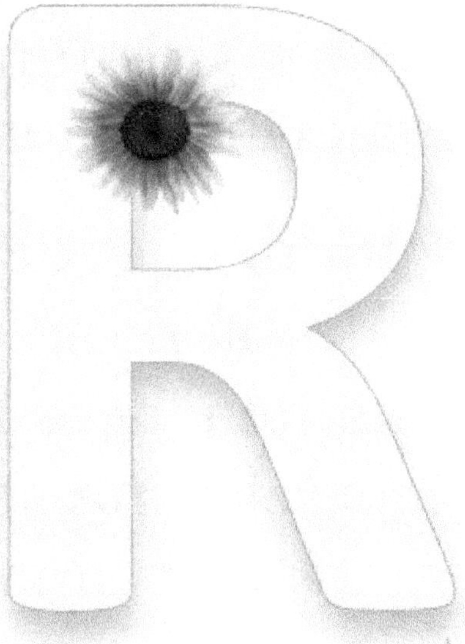

TEACHER...

REIGNING STAR

Teachers are shining, shimmering, splendid.

This pandemic, despite teacher blaming and shaming, teachers regain their reigning star through their sincerity and perseverance.

The Author

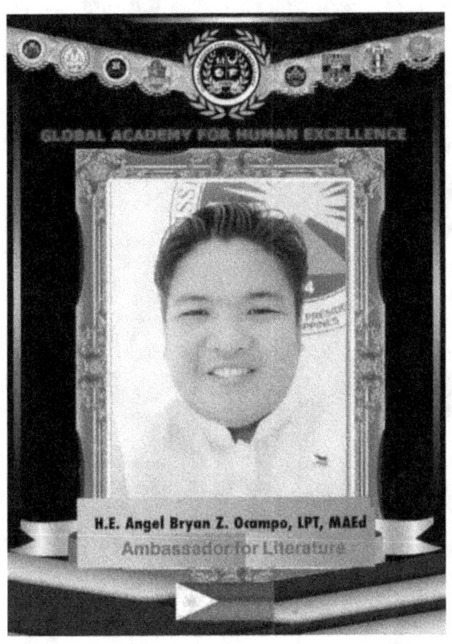

Angel Bryan Z. Ocampo is the author of Silver Lining and Rainbow Gazing, two inspirational self-help books published to spread positivity, kindness, hope, faith and love amidst pandemic.

He is happily married to a fellow teacher, Leny S. Ocampo. He is a father of two adorable sons, Rabbi Samuel and Raziel Schuyler.

He has received the World's Best Teacher Award 2020 from Asian University International (AUI – Model United Nations) on 5th of October 2020 in the Republic of Indonesia.

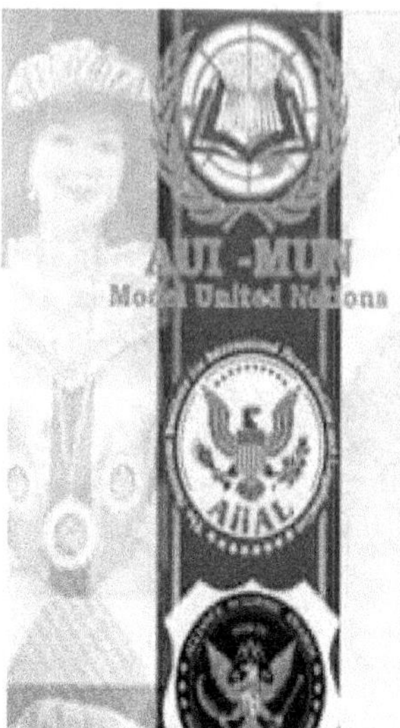

Asian University International

AUI - Model United Nations

AUI support the United Nation in celebrating the World Teachers Day with the theme "Teachers: Leading in Crisis, Reimagining the Future"

World's Best Teacher Award 2020

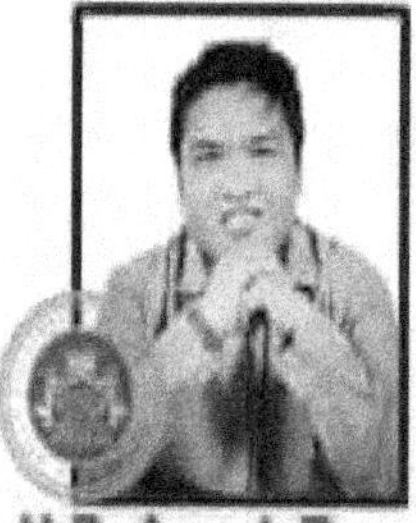

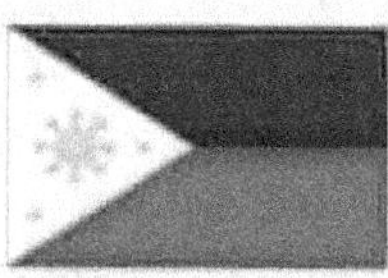

Philippines

H.E. Angel Bryan Z. Ocampo, MAEd, LPT

Teachers have inspired and made a difference to their students lives, they deserve to be celebrated. They have made an outstanding contribution to their profession. Done this 5th of Oct. 2020, in Republic of Indonesia.

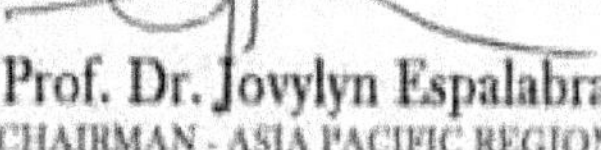

Prof. Dr. Jovylyn Espalabra
CHAIRMAN - ASIA PACIFIC REGION

Prof. Dr. A. Djatmiko Armadi
VICE FOUNDER & CHAIRMAN

Prof. Dr. Bambang Suryanto
FOUNDER & CHAIRMAN

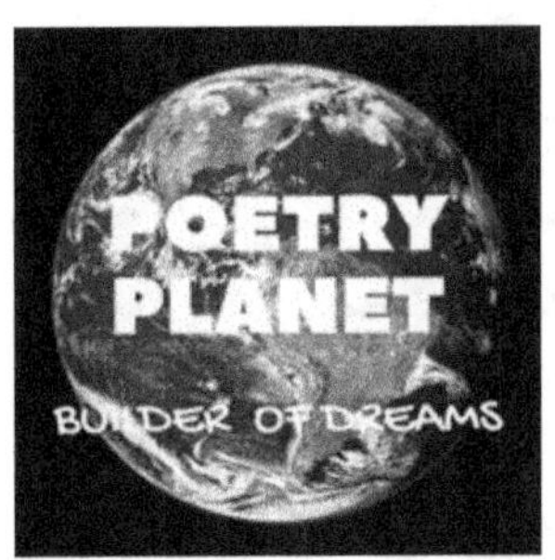

POETRY
PLANET
BUILDER OF DREAMS

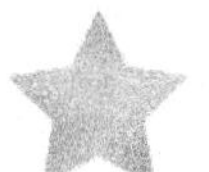

www.ingramcontent.com/pod-product-compliance
Lightning Source LLC
Chambersburg PA
CBHW071353130726
47996CB00002B/910